MAD LIBS®

World's Greatest Word Game

By Roger Price & Leonard Stern

Based on the ◉CBS T

PRICE STERN SLOAN

MAD LIBS®
INSTRUCTIONS

MAD LIBS® is a game for people who don't like games!
It can be played by one, two, three, four, or forty.

• RIDICULOUSLY SIMPLE DIRECTIONS

In this tablet you will find stories containing blank spaces where words are
left out. One player, the READER, selects one of these stories. The READER
does not tell anyone what the story is about. Instead, he/she asks the other
players, the WRITERS, to give him/her words. These words are used to fill
in the blank spaces in the story.

• TO PLAY

The READER asks each WRITER in turn to call out a word—an adjective or
a noun or whatever the space calls for—and uses them to fill in the blank
spaces in the story. The result is a MAD LIBS® game.

When the READER then reads the completed MAD LIBS® game to the other
players, they will discover that they have written a story that is fantastic,
screamingly funny, shocking, silly, crazy, or just plain dumb—depending
upon which words each WRITER called out.

• EXAMPLE (*Before* and *After*)

" _____ !" he said _____
      EXCLAMATION   ADVERB

as he jumped into his convertible _____ and
                              NOUN

drove off with his _____ wife.
              ADJECTIVE

" *Ouch!* !" he said *Stupidly*
      EXCLAMATION   ADVERB

as he jumped into his convertible *cat* and
                              NOUN

drove off with his *brave* wife.
              ADJECTIVE

MAD LIBS®
QUICK REVIEW

In case you have forgotten what adjectives, adverbs, nouns, and verbs are, here is a quick review:

An ADJECTIVE describes something or somebody. *Lumpy, soft, ugly, messy,* and *short* are adjectives.

An ADVERB tells how something is done. It modifies a verb and usually ends in "ly." *Modestly, stupidly, greedily,* and *carefully* are adverbs.

A NOUN is the name of a person, place, or thing. *Sidewalk, umbrella, bridle, bathtub,* and *nose* are nouns.

A VERB is an action word. *Run, pitch, jump,* and *swim* are verbs. Put the verbs in past tense if the directions say PAST TENSE. *Ran, pitched, jumped,* and *swam* are verbs in the past tense.

When we ask for A PLACE, we mean any sort of place: a country or city *(Spain, Cleveland)* or a room *(bathroom, kitchen).*

An EXCLAMATION or SILLY WORD is any sort of funny sound, gasp, grunt, or outcry, like *Wow!, Ouch!, Whomp!, Ick!,* and *Gadzooks!*

When we ask for specific words, like a NUMBER, a COLOR, an ANIMAL, or a PART OF THE BODY, we mean a word that is one of those things, like *seven, blue, horse,* or *head.*

When we ask for a PLURAL, it means more than one. For example, *cat* pluralized is *cats.*

MAD LIBS® is fun to play with friends, but you can also play it by yourself! To begin with, DO NOT look at the story on the page below. Fill in the blanks on this page with the words called for. Then, using the words you have selected, fill in the blank spaces in the story.

Now you've created your own hilarious MAD LIBS® game!

OUTWIT, OUTPLAY, OUTLAST

NUMBER _____

VERB _____

ADVERB_____

PLURAL NOUN _____

VERB _____

ADJECTIVE_____

ADJECTIVE_____

NOUN _____

VERB ENDING IN "ING" _____

PLURAL NOUN _____

MAD LIBS
OUTWIT, OUTPLAY, OUTLAST

Would you live on a deserted island with _____

NUMBER

complete strangers for forty days? I didn't think so! What if you had

to _____ your own food, fight _____

VERB   ADVERB

to stay alive, and constantly run the risk of your new

_____ turning on you? No again, right? Now—what if

PLURAL NOUN

the prize for being the Sole Survivor on the island was one million

dollars? I bet that caught your interest! That's what the contestants

on *Survivor* are there for. They are braving the elements and

learning to _____ nature, all for a/an _____ cash

VERB   ADJECTIVE

prize! All the players are tough and _____ and eager to

ADJECTIVE

win, but only one goes home with the _____. And how

NOUN

do you win it? Working hard and _____ well are two

VERB ENDING IN "ING"

important _____ to have. On this show, only the strong

PLURAL NOUN

survive!

From SURVIVOR™ MAD LIBS® • Survivor © 2004 Survivor Productions, LLC. Copyright © 2004 by Price Stern
Sloan, a division of Penguin Young Readers Group, 345 Hudson Street, New York, New York 10014.

MAD LIBS® is fun to play with friends, but you can also play it by yourself! To begin with, DO NOT look at the story on the page below. Fill in the blanks on this page with the words called for. Then, using the words you have selected, fill in the blank spaces in the story.

Now you've created your own hilarious MAD LIBS® game!

THE RACE IS ON!

VERB _____

ADJECTIVE _____

ADVERB _____

VERB _____

PLURAL NOUN _____

VERB _____

ADJECTIVE _____

ADJECTIVE _____

VERB _____

ADJECTIVE _____

MAD LIBS
THE RACE IS ON!

On the first day, your team will be assigned. You don't get to

_____ who else is on your team, so you should hope
     VERB

you get a/an _____ group of people! People who are
         ADJECTIVE

slow and clumsy or who work _____ are not good additions
          ADVERB

to a team, because they will _____ you in challenges
        VERB

when you are trying to find food and _____. However,
        PLURAL NOUN

you don't want skilled forest rangers either, because your goal is to

_____, and they will have a/an _____
   VERB   ADJECTIVE

advantage over you in the long run. And some people are just

_____. They might appear friendly, but they are
   ADJECTIVE

manipulative and sneaky and will lie and _____ to win the
           VERB

game. So here's a hint: Don't trust any of your _____
           ADJECTIVE

teammates. Good luck!

MAD LIBS® is fun to play with friends, but you can also play it by yourself! To begin with, DO NOT look at the story on the page below. Fill in the blanks on this page with the words called for. Then, using the words you have selected, fill in the blank spaces in the story.

Now you've created your own hilarious MAD LIBS® game!

WAR OF THE WORLDS

NOUN _____

ADVERB _____

PLURAL NOUN _____

VERB _____

NOUN _____

NOUN _____

VERB _____

NUMBER _____

ADJECTIVE _____

VERB _____

PLURAL NOUN _____

NOUN _____

All is fair in love and _____ —and in *Survivor*! Tribes
NOUN

compete against each other fiercely and _____ to win at
ADVERB

challenges and to gain _____. The problem with learning
PLURAL NOUN

to _____ your tribe is that if you lose the Immunity
VERB

_____, one member must get voted off the island! This is a
NOUN

great _____ for a tribe to fight hard to _____
NOUN   VERB

all the challenges. Once you get to day _____, the two
NUMBER

tribes merge, which makes it much more _____. The
ADJECTIVE

people you used to love and _____ are now your enemies,
VERB

while your rivals and _____ are now in your tribe! There
PLURAL NOUN

are so many constant changes that you should always be prepared

for a new _____. And don't trust your friends. They may
NOUN

be foes tomorrow!

MAD LIBS® is fun to play with friends, but you can also play it by yourself! To begin with, DO NOT look at the story on the page below. Fill in the blanks on this page with the words called for. Then, using the words you have selected, fill in the blank spaces in the story.

Now you've created your own hilarious MAD LIBS® game!

HOME ON THE RANGE

ADJECTIVE _____

A PLACE _____

PLURAL NOUN _____

VERB _____

ADJECTIVE _____

ADJECTIVE _____

NOUN _____

NOUN _____

VERB _____

ADJECTIVE _____

VERB _____

PLURAL NOUN _____

ADVERB _____

VERB _____

TYPE OF BUILDING _____

MAD LIBS
HOME ON THE RANGE

Building a/an _____ shelter on the _____
                    ADJECTIVE   A PLACE

is very important to protect you from tropical rainstorms and

_____. Plus, it's nice to _____ under a
   PLURAL NOUN   VERB

roof at night! However, creating the shelter is very _____.
                                                          ADJECTIVE

Building materials may be _____ in the area, and every-
                                ADJECTIVE

one in your _____ will have a different idea of what
                  NOUN

your new home should look like. Location for the _____
                                                        NOUN

is key. If you _____ the shelter on _____
                    VERB   ADJECTIVE

ground, a single downpour might make it flood or _____.
                                                       VERB

Building on sand is also dangerous. If you're lucky enough to win

_____ in a Reward Challenge, you will be able to
   PLURAL NOUN

build more _____, but it's still hard work. You can
                 ADVERB

_____ a teepee, a log cabin, or a/an _____.
   VERB   TYPE OF BUILDING

Just make sure it doesn't collapse while you're inside!

MAD LIBS® is fun to play with friends, but you can also play it by yourself! To begin with, DO NOT look at the story on the page below. Fill in the blanks on this page with the words called for. Then, using the words you have selected, fill in the blank spaces in the story.

Now you've created your own hilarious MAD LIBS® game!

THE *SURVIVOR* DINER

ADJECTIVE_____

NOUN _____

ANIMAL (PLURAL) _____

VERB _____

ADJECTIVE_____

NOUN _____

VERB ENDING IN "ING" _____

PLURAL NOUN _____

ADJECTIVE_____

PLURAL NOUN _____

VERB _____

SAME PLURAL NOUN _____

VERB ENDING IN "ING" _____

ADJECTIVE_____

MAD LIBS
THE *SURVIVOR* DINER

Come on in and take a table: Dinner is served at the *Survivor* Diner!

The _____ main course this evening is seafood.
       ADJECTIVE

Since the beautiful _____ is only a short stroll away, our
                          NOUN

table is full of shellfish, crabs, and delicious _____.
                                                   ANIMAL (PLURAL)

Okay, maybe not completely full . . . whatever you eat, you have to

_____ it yourself! _____ native fruits and
       VERB   ADJECTIVE

plants are also on the menu, but you need nourishing

_____, so you might want to spend more time fishing
     NOUN

and _____ than picking _____. Winning
    VERB ENDING IN "ING"   PLURAL NOUN

a/an _____ challenge might get you a supply of
            ADJECTIVE

_____, which are high-energy and delicious. Don't
     PLURAL NOUN

_____ too much, though, because the more
              VERB

_____ you eat now, the less you'll have later. And the
   SAME PLURAL NOUN

more time you spend _____, the less time you will
                          VERB ENDING IN "ING"

have for figuring out your _____ Tree Mail!
                                  ADJECTIVE

MAD LIBS® is fun to play with friends, but you can also play it by yourself! To begin with, DO NOT look at the story on the page below. Fill in the blanks on this page with the words called for. Then, using the words you have selected, fill in the blank spaces in the story.

Now you've created your own hilarious MAD LIBS® game!

PUZZLE IT OUT

ADJECTIVE_____

VERB _____

ADVERB_____

FOREIGN LANGUAGE _____

PLURAL NOUN _____

ADJECTIVE_____

VERB _____

ADJECTIVE_____

VERB _____

VERB _____

MAD LIBS
PUZZLE IT OUT

You might think word games are calm and _____
                                              ADJECTIVE

games, but since it's *Survivor*, there's always a twist! Players race to

_____ a bunch of letters as _____ as
        VERB   ADVERB

they can. The hard part? There are lots of extra letters from the

_____ alphabet! Some of the letters are hanging from
FOREIGN LANGUAGE

trees, covered with _____, so you can't see which ones
                         PLURAL NOUN

you need. Some are at the ends of _____ ropes that you
                                        ADJECTIVE

have to _____ before you can read them. Some are in
            VERB

a/an _____ dish of other letters, just waiting for you to
        ADJECTIVE

_____ them out. Once you've gathered them all, you
        VERB

have to _____ a certain word to win the challenge. So have
            VERB

fun—but don't get puzzled!

MAD LIBS® is fun to play with friends, but you can also play it by yourself! To begin with, DO NOT look at the story on the page below. Fill in the blanks on this page with the words called for. Then, using the words you have selected, fill in the blank spaces in the story.

Now you've created your own hilarious MAD LIBS® game!

RIDING THE WAVES

OCCUPATION _____

VERB _____

ADJECTIVE _____

VERB _____

NOUN _____

NUMBER _____

ADJECTIVE _____

VERB _____

NOUN _____

VERB _____

ADJECTIVE _____

MAD LIBS
RIDING THE WAVES

This stunt is made for you if you're a swimmer or _____.
                                                    OCCUPATION

Two tribes have to _____ against each other to see
                        VERB

which one can complete the _____ course first—but
                                ADJECTIVE

the whole course is on water! First, _____ along a
                                          VERB

balance beam from one float to another. Don't fall in! Then jump

into the _____ and untie _____ paddles.
              NOUN   NUMBER

Remember, it might be more _____ to untie the knots
                                ADJECTIVE

when they are wet. Join your teammate and _____
                                                VERB

some barrels, then meet the next teammate and untie one more

_____. Swim to shore, then _____ your
     NOUN   VERB

boat into the water. It might be _____, so push hard.
                                      ADJECTIVE

Then paddle back to the starting point. Are you ready? Jump in!

MAD LIBS® is fun to play with friends, but you can also play it by yourself! To begin with, DO NOT look at the story on the page below. Fill in the blanks on this page with the words called for. Then, using the words you have selected, fill in the blank spaces in the story.

Now you've created your own hilarious MAD LIBS® game!

THE CHALLENGES

ADJECTIVE _____

ADJECTIVE _____

PLURAL NOUN _____

VERB _____

PLURAL NOUN _____

ADJECTIVE _____

NUMBER _____

VERB _____

NOUN _____

FOREIGN COUNTRY _____

TYPE OF FOOD (PLURAL) _____

ADJECTIVE _____

ADVERB _____

MAD LIBS
THE CHALLENGES

There are two kinds of _____ challenges in *Survivor*:
                          ADJECTIVE

the Reward Challenge and the Immunity Challenge. Both are

_____ and very exciting, but they give you very different
ADJECTIVE

_____ if you win them. Winning the Immunity
     PLURAL NOUN

Challenge will _____ you immunity for the next Tribal
                    VERB

Council—the best possible gift to you and your team! If the

_____ have already merged, you are safe from the vote
     PLURAL NOUN

at _____ Council, and if they haven't, your whole team
     ADJECTIVE

has to stay on the island for another _____ days. Either way,
                                        NUMBER

you can _____! If you win the Reward Challenge, you get a
          VERB

special _____ that no one else on the island can have, like
          NOUN

a phone call to your aunt from _____ or a delicious plate
                                 FOREIGN COUNTRY

of _____. But be careful. The more _____
   TYPE OF FOOD (PLURAL)   ADJECTIVE

the prize, the more jealous your tribemates will be of you. So don't

show off. Just enjoy your reward _____. That might be the
                                    ADVERB

most challenging part of all!

MAD LIBS® is fun to play with friends, but you can also play it by yourself! To begin with, DO NOT look at the story on the page below. Fill in the blanks on this page with the words called for. Then, using the words you have selected, fill in the blank spaces in the story.

Now you've created your own hilarious MAD LIBS® game!

SURVIVOR R & R

ADJECTIVE _____

TYPE OF FOOD (PLURAL) _____

VERB _____

NOUN _____

ADJECTIVE _____

VERB _____

PLURAL NOUN _____

TYPE OF BUILDING _____

VERB ENDING IN "ING" _____

PLURAL NOUN _____

ADJECTIVE _____

NOUN _____

Between completing _____ challenges and scavenging
                         ADJECTIVE

for _____, the contestants like to rest and
      TYPE OF FOOD (PLURAL)

_____ a little. Some favorite activities are napping,
       VERB

swimming, and lying out in the _____. Every player has
                                      NOUN

a/an _____ activity of choice, though; some people
        ADJECTIVE

play sand-golf, while others _____ for much of the day.
                                    VERB

Other contestants like to keep useful, and in their free time they

might sharpen their _____ or build a convenient
                          PLURAL NOUN

_____ for the tribe's boats. Or the whole tribe might
   TYPE OF BUILDING

participate in _____ songs around the fire at night or
                VERB ENDING IN "ING"

drawing _____ on one another. Whatever you're doing,
          PLURAL NOUN

don't be alone for too long—every minute you're _____
                                                        ADJECTIVE

is another minute for your tribemates to form a/an _____
                                                          NOUN

against you!

MAD LIBS® is fun to play with friends, but you can also play it by yourself! To begin with, DO NOT look at the story on the page below. Fill in the blanks on this page with the words called for. Then, using the words you have selected, fill in the blank spaces in the story.

Now you've created your own hilarious MAD LIBS® game!

THE ANTHROPOLOGIST, PART I

NUMBER _____

ADJECTIVE_____

SILLY WORD_____

SILLY WORD_____

ADJECTIVE_____

VERB _____

TYPE OF FOOD (PLURAL) _____

ADJECTIVE_____

VERB ENDING IN "ING" _____

PLURAL NOUN _____

NOUN _____

ADJECTIVE_____

MAD LIBS
THE ANTHROPOLOGIST, PART I

I am a scientist who has been working in this region for

_____ years, and never before have I seen so
      NUMBER

_____ a group of natives! They seem to be in two tribes,
  ADJECTIVE

called the _____ and the _____, and
      SILLY WORD   SILLY WORD

they speak a strange and _____ language. They _____
            ADJECTIVE   VERB

all day and eat local foods like _____, which they gather
               TYPE OF FOOD (PLURAL)

from the forests surrounding them. Men and women work together

in harmony. The natives form _____ alliances and seem to
         ADJECTIVE

enjoy _____ with one another. They wear matching
  VERB ENDING IN "ING"

_____ on their heads, which seems to indicate the
  PLURAL NOUN

_____ they are part of. This advanced civilization is
  NOUN

quite a discovery—I can't wait to write a/an _____
                              ADJECTIVE

book about them or maybe even a TV show!

MAD LIBS® is fun to play with friends, but you can also play it by yourself! To begin with, DO NOT look at the story on the page below. Fill in the blanks on this page with the words called for. Then, using the words you have selected, fill in the blank spaces in the story.

Now you've created your own hilarious MAD LIBS® game!

THE ANTHROPOLOGIST, PART II

ADJECTIVE_____

SILLY WORD_____

ADVERB_____

VERB _____

NOUN _____

ADJECTIVE_____

VERB ENDING IN "ING" _____

SILLY WORD_____

FOREIGN COUNTRY _____

PLURAL NOUN _____

VERB _____

VERB _____

ADJECTIVE_____

I am currently witnessing a/an _____ development in
ADJECTIVE

my tribe, which I have decided to call the _____. One
SILLY WORD

by one, the natives are disappearing! They seem to have a ritual in

which they _____ determine, using democratic methods,
ADVERB

which tribe member will _____ next. The member
VERB

elected to go has his or her symbolic _____ put out,
NOUN

then walks off into the wilderness. What a/an _____
ADJECTIVE

government system for such a primitive tribe! Recently, they have

been _____ in races and contests, much like the
VERB ENDING IN "ING"

_____ tribe of _____. They row boats,
SILLY WORD   FOREIGN COUNTRY

run _____, and lift heavy objects for no apparent reason!
PLURAL NOUN

The other day, I watched them _____ giant masks and
VERB

_____ with them. Perhaps they were making a sacrifice
VERB

to their _____ gods. How strange!
ADJECTIVE

MAD LIBS® is fun to play with friends, but you can also play it by yourself! To begin with, DO NOT look at the story on the page below. Fill in the blanks on this page with the words called for. Then, using the words you have selected, fill in the blank spaces in the story.

Now you've created your own hilarious MAD LIBS® game!

SQUEAKY CLEAN

ADJECTIVE_____

NOUN _____

VERB _____

PLURAL NOUN _____

ADJECTIVE_____

NOUN _____

ADJECTIVE_____

VERB _____

PART OF THE BODY _____

ADJECTIVE_____

VERB _____

PART OF THE BODY _____

SQUEAKY CLEAN

Everyone loves that _____ feeling you get after a long,
                          ADJECTIVE

hot shower. So what about the *Survivor* contestants, who don't even

have plumbing on their _____? Keeping clean is a
                              NOUN

real challenge on the island! The ocean looks like a good place to

_____ in and clean yourself, but it's so full of
      VERB

_____ that you might feel dirtier after you climb out!
   PLURAL NOUN

You might have to find a/an _____ stream or
                                  ADJECTIVE

_____ farther inland on the island, where there will be
      NOUN

less _____ salt. There's still no soap to _____
       ADJECTIVE   VERB

with, though, so bring a friend to scrub your _____!
                                                  PART OF THE BODY

Toothpaste is also difficult to find on a/an _____
                                                    ADJECTIVE

tropical island, so you might want to _____ your teeth
                                            VERB

with sand instead. And the toothbrush? Your _____, of
                                                PART OF THE BODY

course! Good luck keeping clean!

MAD LIBS® is fun to play with friends, but you can also play it by yourself! To begin with, DO NOT look at the story on the page below. Fill in the blanks on this page with the words called for. Then, using the words you have selected, fill in the blank spaces in the story.

Now you've created your own hilarious MAD LIBS® game!

JUNGLE GYM

ADJECTIVE_____

NOUN _____

PLURAL NOUN _____

NUMBER _____

VERB _____

ADVERB_____

ADJECTIVE_____

ADJECTIVE_____

VERB _____

NOUN _____

MAD LIBS
JUNGLE GYM

Some *Survivor* challenges can be a real workout. This is one for

the _____ bodybuilders! An uncomfortable wooden
        ADJECTIVE

_____ is laid across your back and the backs of two of
        NOUN

your teammates and three _____ from the rival tribe.
                              PLURAL NOUN

The team will take turns putting _____-pound weights on
                                      NUMBER

each side of the pole. _____ your strategy _____:
                            VERB   ADVERB

Do you want to weigh down the strong or the _____
                                                      ADJECTIVE

first? Or maybe you plan to distribute the weights evenly to make it

_____ for the whole team? Hold onto that pole. If you
        ADJECTIVE

_____ it, the game is over! The goal is to be the last
        VERB

_____ with a man—or woman—standing. Only the
        NOUN

strong survive!

MAD LIBS® is fun to play with friends, but you can also play it by yourself! To begin with, DO NOT look at the story on the page below. Fill in the blanks on this page with the words called for. Then, using the words you have selected, fill in the blank spaces in the story.

Now you've created your own hilarious MAD LIBS® game!

BLUE'S CLUES

SOMETHING ALIVE (PLURAL) _____

ADJECTIVE_____

TYPE OF FOOD (PLURAL) _____

PLURAL NOUN _____

VERB ENDING IN "ING" _____

VERB _____

ADJECTIVE_____

ADJECTIVE_____

PLURAL NOUN _____

SAME PLURAL NOUN _____

VERB (PAST TENSE)_____

ADVERB_____

MAD LIBS
BLUE'S CLUES

Eating seafood and _____ can get _____

                            SOMETHING ALIVE (PLURAL)   ADJECTIVE

very fast. If you're lucky, the host will have a special stash of more

interesting food lined up for you, like rice or _____.

                                                      TYPE OF FOOD (PLURAL)

And it's always good to have some backup _____, in

                                              PLURAL NOUN

case you run out of food or have a bad day _____

                                               VERB ENDING IN "ING"

fish. However, you've got to _____ if you want to find

                                    VERB

this _____ feast! A box of _____ food is

      ADJECTIVE   ADJECTIVE

in your tribe's camp, but to get to the contents, you have to win

challenges and earn _____. Once you have enough

                              PLURAL NOUN

_____, open the box—and enjoy the delicious food

SAME PLURAL NOUN

you've _____ so hard for. Save some for later, even

                   VERB (PAST TENSE)

though you'll be tempted to eat it all _____. The fruits of

                                                   ADVERB

labor are sweet!

MAD LIBS® is fun to play with friends, but you can also play it by yourself! To begin with, DO NOT look at the story on the page below. Fill in the blanks on this page with the words called for. Then, using the words you have selected, fill in the blank spaces in the story.

Now you've created your own hilarious MAD LIBS® game!

SURVIVOR ON THE RUNWAY

ADJECTIVE_____

CELEBRITY (FEMALE)_____

CELEBRITY (MALE)_____

ADJECTIVE_____

COLOR_____

PLURAL NOUN _____

ADJECTIVE_____

VERB ENDING IN "ING" _____

ANIMAL _____

PART OF THE BODY_____

NOUN _____

NOUN _____

EXCLAMATION_____

The *Survivor* fashion statement is definitely the most _____
                                                          ADJECTIVE

on television. Everyone is following the *Survivor* trend, even big

stars like _____ and _____! The style for
           CELEBRITY (FEMALE)   CELEBRITY (MALE)

women is simple, chic, and _____. Short shorts and
                            ADJECTIVE

cute _____ tops are the way to go. Men will wear
          COLOR

longer _____ but might take off their shirts to get a/an
         PLURAL NOUN

_____ tan. If you're going _____ or want
   ADJECTIVE   VERB ENDING IN "ING"

to catch a/an _____, something to keep your hair off
                   ANIMAL

your _____ might come in handy. It will also be useful
         PART OF THE BODY

for wiping _____ off your face if the weather is hot—
                NOUN

which it almost always is. You can wear sneakers or sandals,

whichever you prefer. Make sure you wear something on your feet,

since you don't want to burn them on the hot _____.
                                                  NOUN

That would most likely make you scream, "_____!"
                                            EXCLAMATION

MAD LIBS® is fun to play with friends, but you can also play it by yourself! To begin with, DO NOT look at the story on the page below. Fill in the blanks on this page with the words called for. Then, using the words you have selected, fill in the blank spaces in the story.

Now you've created your own hilarious MAD LIBS® game!

I DEMAND A RECOUNT!

NOUN _____

NUMBER _____

ADJECTIVE_____

NOUN _____

VERB _____

PART OF THE BODY _____

VERB ENDING IN "ING" _____

PLURAL NOUN _____

NOUN _____

VERB _____

ADJECTIVE_____

MAD LIBS
I DEMAND A RECOUNT!

As if life on the island wasn't hard enough, there's another

_____ to deal with on *Survivor*. Every _____
NOUN   NUMBER

days, there is a chance you will get kicked off! There is no

_____ way to make sure you stay on the _____,
ADJECTIVE   NOUN

unless you win immunity for every Tribal Council. Since that isn't

going to _____, you've got to learn to play the game.
                 VERB

Keep your _____ on the other players at all times to
            PART OF THE BODY

make sure they aren't _____ against you. Try to
                VERB ENDING IN "ING"

make friends of your _____, but don't trust every
               PLURAL NOUN

_____ they say, because they may be lying to keep them-
NOUN

selves on the island. Do favors for the other players, so they will

_____ you, but don't let them think you're _____.
VERB   ADJECTIVE

Play fair, but not too fair!

From SURVIVOR™ MAD LIBS® • Survivor © 2004 Survivor Productions, LLC. Copyright © 2004 by Price Stern
Sloan, a division of Penguin Young Readers Group, 345 Hudson Street, New York, New York 10014.

MAD LIBS® is fun to play with friends, but you can also play it by yourself! To begin with, DO NOT look at the story on the page below. Fill in the blanks on this page with the words called for. Then, using the words you have selected, fill in the blank spaces in the story.

Now you've created your own hilarious MAD LIBS® game!

BUG BUFFET

VERB (PAST TENSE)_____

NOUN _____

PLURAL NOUN _____

PLURAL NOUN _____

VERB _____

VERB ENDING IN "ING" _____

ADJECTIVE_____

SOMETHING ALIVE (PLURAL) _____

ADJECTIVE_____

One of the most shocking challenges on *Survivor* wasn't even

_____ by the players—their *relatives* were forced to
VERB (PAST TENSE)

compete in an icky, sticky bug-eating contest! The Survivors' loved

ones were flown to the _____ to see their sons,
NOUN

_____, boyfriends, wives, and _____ whom
PLURAL NOUN   PLURAL NOUN

they'd missed for so long. The catch? To spend time with the

Survivors they loved, they would have to _____ giant
VERB

roaches! The Survivors were cheering and _____ as
VERB ENDING IN "ING"

the _____ competition progressed. The loved one who
ADJECTIVE

ate the most _____ was allowed to spend time
SOMETHING ALIVE (PLURAL)

with the Survivor he or she had missed. You can bet they weren't

_____ fans of the local cuisine!
ADJECTIVE

MAD LIBS® is fun to play with friends, but you can also play it by yourself! To begin with, DO NOT look at the story on the page below. Fill in the blanks on this page with the words called for. Then, using the words you have selected, fill in the blank spaces in the story.

Now you've created your own hilarious MAD LIBS® game!

A RELAXING TROPICAL VACATION

ADJECTIVE _____

VERB _____

NOUN _____

PLURAL NOUN _____

ADVERB _____

VERB _____

ANIMAL (PLURAL) _____

NOUN _____

ADJECTIVE _____

ADJECTIVE _____

MAD LIBS
A RELAXING
TROPICAL VACATION

Are you stressed-out? Working too hard? _____ when
                                              ADJECTIVE

you get up in the morning? Sounds like you need a relaxing trip to a

Survivor Island to rejuvenate and _____ you! Your
                                            VERB

_____ will be from three to thirty-nine days, depending
      NOUN

on how well you get along with your _____.
                                            PLURAL NOUN

The food is all _____ prepared—by you and your
                      ADVERB

friends—and you have the chance to _____ your own
                                            VERB

house just the way you like it! Local wildlife, like monkeys and

_____, live right in your backyard or even inside your
   ANIMAL (PLURAL)

_____! Swimming in the _____ ocean
      NOUN   ADJECTIVE

and playing fun games for prizes are only some of the exciting

activities we offer here. Don't bother packing much. You can't take it

with you on this _____ island. Sign up here for
                        ADJECTIVE

Survivor—a relaxing tropical vacation!

From SURVIVOR™ MAD LIBS® • Survivor © 2004 Survivor Productions, LLC. Copyright © 2004 by Price Stern
Sloan, a division of Penguin Young Readers Group, 345 Hudson Street, New York, New York 10014.

MAD LIBS® is fun to play with friends, but you can also play it by yourself! To begin with, DO NOT look at the story on the page below. Fill in the blanks on this page with the words called for. Then, using the words you have selected, fill in the blank spaces in the story.

Now you've created your own hilarious MAD LIBS® game!

GONE FISHING

TYPE OF PLANT (PLURAL) _____

NOUN _____

PLURAL NOUN _____

VERB _____

ADJECTIVE _____

ADJECTIVE _____

VERB _____

NOUN _____

NOUN _____

ADJECTIVE _____

ADVERB _____

Do you know how to fish? I hope so! If not, you'll be stuck eating

_____ all day! Fishing is a major activity on the
TYPE OF PLANT (PLURAL)

_____ and may take up a lot of your time. Nets, spears,
NOUN

fishing rods, and _____ can all be used, but you might
PLURAL NOUN

have to win some challenges to _____ them. The types
VERB

of fish around the island are _____; most are friendly,
ADJECTIVE

but be careful of stingrays, sharks, and even _____
ADJECTIVE

piranhas! You may have to _____ your boat out to sea
VERB

to catch enough fish for your whole _____. Shellfish
NOUN

can be found on the _____ in many varieties. There
NOUN

are mussels and crabs, and squid may be washed up on the beach

during _____ tide. Gather them up _____—
ADJECTIVE   ADVERB

If there's not enough for dinner, your tribe will be pretty crabby!

From SURVIVOR™ MAD LIBS® • Survivor © 2004 Survivor Productions, LLC. Copyright © 2004 by Price Stern
Sloan, a division of Penguin Young Readers Group, 345 Hudson Street, New York, New York 10014.

MAD LIBS® is fun to play with friends, but you can also play it by yourself! To begin with, DO NOT look at the story on the page below. Fill in the blanks on this page with the words called for. Then, using the words you have selected, fill in the blank spaces in the story.

Now you've created your own hilarious MAD LIBS® game!

SOLE *SURVIVOR*

ADJECTIVE_____

VERB _____

NOUN _____

VERB _____

ADJECTIVE_____

ADJECTIVE_____

VERB _____

VERB _____

MAD LIBS
SOLE *SURVIVOR*

So you want to be Sole *Survivor*? You've got a lot of work to do!

There are three _____ strategies to use if you want to
                          ADJECTIVE

_____. Pick whichever works best for you. You can use
        VERB

honesty, trickery, or the compromise of _____. The problem
                                                NOUN

with honesty is that everyone can lie to you and _____
                                                        VERB

you, so you won't know which alliances are _____.
                                                    ADJECTIVE

The problem with trickery is the opposite. You will have lied to so

many _____ people that no one will _____ you,
          ADJECTIVE   VERB

and the people in the Jury at the final decision will not be your

biggest fans! The best strategy, then, is to _____ as much
                                                    VERB

as you have to but be honest, too: In the end, the Jury just might

choose you to be Sole *Survivor*!

MAD LIBS® is fun to play with friends, but you can also play it by yourself! To begin with, DO NOT look at the story on the page below. Fill in the blanks on this page with the words called for. Then, using the words you have selected, fill in the blank spaces in the story.

Now you've created your own hilarious MAD LIBS® game!

WILD WILDLIFE

A PLACE _____

ADJECTIVE_____

VERB _____

ANIMAL (PLURAL) _____

ADJECTIVE_____

ADJECTIVE_____

PLURAL NOUN _____

PLURAL NOUN _____

ADJECTIVE_____

ANIMAL (PLURAL) _____

MAD LIBS
WILD WILDLIFE

Do you have dreams of a career at the zoo, the circus, or the

_____? If so, *Survivor* might be a/an _____
    A PLACE   ADJECTIVE

place for you! There are animals galore on the island that you can

_____ with every day. Monkeys, bats, and _____
    VERB   ANIMAL (PLURAL)

are some of the most _____ mammals, while alligators
                                ADJECTIVE

and snakes make up the _____ reptile population. Rare
                                ADJECTIVE

birds compete with you for the _____ washed up on the
                                PLURAL NOUN

beach, and toucans and sloths watch you from the trees. With so

many _____, it's not a surprise when some animals become
      PLURAL NOUN

pets—Pelican Pete and Balboa the Snake both became

_____ friends with the *Survivors*. Hey, they may not
    ADJECTIVE

be cute, cuddly _____, but beggars can't be choosers!
                ANIMAL (PLURAL)